LESSONS FOR THE #JOURNEY

BY
PAULA BLACKWELL, KYMONE HINDS &
PHILIP M. WESLEY II

Watersprings
PUBLISHING

Lessons for the Journey
Published by
Watersprings Media House, LLC.
P.O. BOX 1284
Olive Branch, MS 38654
www.waterspringsmedia.com

Contact publisher for bulk orders and permission requests.

Library of Congress Control Number: 2018964797

ISBN 13: 978-1-948877-16-9

Table of Contents

TABLE OF CONTENTS

#LESSONS LEARNED

I am a teacher, it's a job I love. I believe that we learn from doing. So, most of my devotionals are from the lessons I've learned. I hope you learn from my hard head and don't make the same mistakes I made.

Peace and Blessings,

Paula Blackwell

@paulaprinciples

NEW YEAR, NEW YOU

Our Reminder Text –

I will stand upon my watch, and set me upon the tower, and will watch to see what he will say unto me, and what I shall answer when I am reproved. And the LORD answered me, and said, Write the vision, and make it plain upon tables, that he may run that readeth it.

Habakkuk 2:1-2 KJV

The beautiful thing about a new year is that it gives each of us a new opportunity to be better than the previous year.

I've read many Facebook posts and Instagram messages on the awesome things people plan for the new year. In looking back over the last several years, I've noticed that there are many occasions where my plans or thoughts weren't even close to what ended up actually happening.

I read a post by my Facebook friend DeVon Franklin he said, " As I sat here in meditation and prayer, I asked God for the same power to walk on water. I know that may sound strange, but I wasn't asking for the literal power but for the metaphorical power which simply means...the power to do the impossible. I want to do what has never been done before in the history of the Earth and I'm bold enough to believe God will answer my prayer!"

I began to realize I have impossible dreams too that are just that, dreams. Why haven't I asked God to make those dreams a reality? Why don't I believe that those dreams can come true? I think many of us are afraid to ask God to do the impossible.

I've decided to take DeVon's advice and ask God for the impossible and watch Him work. We have not, because we ask not. If you've always wanted to be a teacher; ask God to make that happen. If you've always wanted to be a mentor; ask Him to make it happen. Write the dream, ask God for the plan and let's make our dreams come true.

God has already promised us that He will give us the desires of our heart. All we have to do is ask. This year I'm asking for the impossible. Will you?

Happy New Year!

MEMORY FAILURES

Our Reminder Text –

Even to your old age and gray hairs I am he, I am he who will sustain you. I have made you and I will carry you; I will sustain you and I will rescue you.

Isaiah 46:4 NIV

I have a confession, I have a bad habit. I wish I could get rid of it. It's something I'm not ashamed to share, however it is something I wish I could get rid of.

I'm a person who recalls tragedy very easily. I've been affected by so many things in my life and I never forget them. My sister said to me "Why can't you just block it out like everyone else". I don't have an answer for her. I don't know why these things stay with me.

Why do I remember every year the day my parents were almost killed - Feb 3? They don't remember, but I never forget. My brother-in-law committed suicide more than 20 years ago the week before Easter. I wish I could forget that. I can't. I see his family and I can't forget.

I remember the day my best friend Kim called me to give me the news my God-mother Mrs. Willis had died. She's had to tell me bad news a couple of times in our lives and I remember exactly what she said every time.

I don't know why I can't block out those things from my memory, but I think it might have something to do with learning how to cope in difficult times. I realized after looking back during those days, I wasn't my normal self. God had given me an extra dose of support to assist those in difficult situations.

It has never occurred to me to block out the bad days. If I did, then I probably would not fully appreciate the good days.

God never promised us all good days, but He sure promised to carry us through those days. I place all I have in His hands. And all of my good days outweigh my bad days, so I won't complain.

#LessonLearned

I AM AN ADDICT

―――――――――

Our Reminder Text –

Peace I leave with you; my peace I give to you. Not as the world gives do I give to you. Let not your hearts be troubled, neither let them be afraid.

John 14:27 ESV

―――――――――

Hello, my name is Paula Sanders Blackwell and I'm a recovering addict. If we are real with ourselves, everyone is recovering from something. I am a food addict. I was completely confused about how I was filling my life with bad food. It filled my loneliness and it filled my celebrations. I am also a recovering control freak. I would often try to control all these things, but not realizing I had no control over anything.

I discovered the power of prayer. I began to lay my burdens down, and guess what? I left them there. I didn't worry over them anymore. I didn't stress over the consequences. I just decided one day to give it to God. Many times, we go to God in prayer and then worry about it too. I realized I couldn't do both, that was a waste of energy.

The lesson I learned was to take it to the Lord in prayer and leave it there. I put it out of my head. I quit sweating myself. My anxiety levels decreased. I do not stress out over many things anymore. I do have to remind myself not to allow people, jobs, money or work to stress me. But it's a lesson I learned the hard way. Choose today - you're either going to pray or stress. I vote to pray.

#LessonLearned

BE CAREFUL WHAT YOU PRAY FOR

Our Reminder Text –

Teach me Your way, O LORD; I will walk in Your truth; Unite my heart to fear Your name.

Psalms 86:11 ESV

Many of my insecurities come from my lack of being able to control a situation. I know I have control issues. I am someone who likes to know every possible outcome. I also understand as a Christian that it is just not possible. I have learned that life will not always go the way I plan it in my head. If you live long enough you will experience something that I call unplanned events.

Unplanned events aren't all bad. There are some wonderful unplanned events. But in my experience, they haven't been exactly wonderful. I didn't plan to get divorced. But God used that situation to teach me patience.

I initially didn't plan to move to Texas. But God used that move to help me grow stronger in His will not my will. In each situation I have learned to pray for His will to be done, not mine.

The lesson here is, be careful what you pray for. Many times, we pray our will and not God's will. I recall praying after an interview that I wanted the job. God answered my prayer, I got the job. However, in the end that job was not what I needed. But my focus was on the salary. I'll never take a job for simply the money. I learned my lesson.

God's will and my will haven't always synced up. I had to Learn how to pray for His leading and then let Him lead. That is hard when you like to control every aspect of your life. I've learned some lessons the easy way and others the hard way, but I'm glad God still finds me worthy of teaching.

#LessonLearned

PAULA BLACKWELL

FIRST LOVES

Our Reminder Text –

"We are hard-pressed on every side, yet not crushed; we are perplexed, but not in despair; persecuted, but not forsaken; struck down, but not destroyed."

2 Corinthians 4:8-9 NIV

Do you recall your first love? Well I remember all of my first loves. I was young and naïve, and I thought all of them were my first loves. I had no idea most of them wouldn't last more than ninety days.

When you're young you don't believe that life will be any different five years from now. And you think the person you're with is going to last forever. I've had my fair share of forevers. But in all of my youth there was only one boy that I told "Please don't call me until you're dead."

The pain the boy caused me at the time was immeasurable. He lied, he cheated, but in the end, I told him to die. In my mind he's still dead. Although I'm told he's living in Delaware.

But I'm sure God in His infinite mercy saw this situation and decided since I never asked His opinion of the boy that I probably needed a lesson in true love. Beautiful lesson. God delivered me from the boy and in the process, I learned a great deal about some people I thought were my friends.

When we live, and act outside God's will for our lives there is no telling what can happen. In hindsight I'm just glad I survived with no permanent damage. He gave me mercy in my stupidity. But one good thing that came out of this foolishness...I didn't need to learn this lesson twice. I got it the first time. I don't know what my former love learned. But I'm guessing he learned a lesson too.

From that day forward, I learned to always take my loves before God. When you go into a relationship with God first, you establish the connection that will be a lifetime friendship. Trust that He will never lead you wrong, all you have to do is listen.

#LessonLearned

A DRAFT LESSON

Our Reminder Text –

Having gifts that differ according to the grace given to us, let us use them: if prophecy, in proportion to our faith; if service, in our serving; the one who teaches, in his teaching; the one who exhorts, in his exhortation; the one who contributes, in generosity; the one who leads, with zeal; the one who does acts of mercy, with cheerfulness."

Romans 12:6-8 ESV

For those of you who follow me on social media, you know I am from Birmingham, Alabama. I'm a huge Alabama Crimson Tide fan, and since I grew up in the south I never paid attention to the National Football League. We didn't have a team in any of the cities in which I lived. My daddy pulled for the New Orleans Saints when we lived in Mobile, Alabama, but It wasn't until I had a former student participate in the NFL draft that I paid attention to the National Football League.

The whole NFL draft process fascinates me. I mean, you have all of these young men, many of whom are African-American, hoping to get drafted by a franchise and become instant millionaires.

What I find interesting is that once they are drafted, most of them always thank their mothers, and a few of them thank God for the opportunity to live out their dreams. But I wonder how many keep that mindset of knowing God deserves the glory throughout their careers. God has given these young men tremendous talent, and I hope they use it wisely. Football is simultaneously dangerous and exciting! I pray for the young men who get drafted into the NFL to use their financial blessings wisely, because a serious enough injury could cause them to stop playing in an instant. I also hope they use their time wisely, because as we get older we realize time isn't our friend and we can't do the same things we used to do, the same way we used to do them.

God gives each of us talent, whether it's excelling on the grid-iron, hardwood, or the baseball field, being able to sing beautifully or being excellent writers. God admonishes us to use our talents for His glory. Are you using your talents for His glory? I discovered my talents a long time ago, and I'm very excited to be using my writing to reach others.

#LessonLearned

AN UNFORGIVING SPIRIT

Our Reminder Text –

**But I say to you, love your enemies
and pray for those who persecute you.**

Matthew 5:44 NIV

I believe in testimonies. But sometimes I think people use testimonial periods to make confessions that probably should be given only to God, or licensed therapists who take oaths of confidentiality.

A few years ago, I was the Praise & Worship leader for a church in metro Atlanta. During a prayer meeting, an elderly woman stood to share her testimony. She was asking the church to pray for her because she had recently lost her husband. She then clarified that although he was legally still her husband, he had left her and her kids many years ago.

Initially, I didn't look up because I was searching for a song to sing during prayer. But when she said, "She was glad he was dead because he'd caused her and her children so much pain," my ears popped open and my head went up. Needless to say, by this time our pastor, and the entire congregation were in shock. The elderly woman went on to share how her estranged husband had mistreated her and her sons, saying he'd run off with other women. Well, as you can imagine there wasn't a sound in that church other than the words coming out of the woman's mouth.

She confessed she felt no pity for him, or the fact that he'd developed Alzheimer's and was hit by a bus. And all the while I kept thinking, *she's got to be joking. She wasn't.*

The text messages started flying around in that church like angels' wings!! What did she say? Did we hear her wrong? Nope. We heard her right. We all did. A few of us tried not to have eye contact with each other because we knew we would start laughing. This woman professed her profound hatred for her husband to the entire church.

We all just sat there in shock. Our poor pastor, he was fairly new to our congregation, and I know he had to be thinking, *"What in the world?"*

I had so many questions. Why would she stay married to the man after he left her? Did she think he might someday come back? Why hadn't she divorced him? A few weeks later I saw the elderly woman in the church bathroom and my curiosity got the better of me, so I asked her, "If you knew he was unfaithful and saw how he had abandoned you and your kids, why didn't you divorce him?"

She said, "I kept waiting on him to divorce me, and I didn't want my children to be hurt."

She admitted that her kids hated him and the way he treated her. But in the end, it was her eldest son who took him in to care for him until the bus accident took his life.

I don't think she realized how much her inability to move on hurt her children. She hadn't moved on with her life, she kept his name and raised his sons while he ran off with other women. She made the choice to not forgive, but simply to ignore.

The unforgiving spirit is dangerous. This woman spent years

hating this man. Her life was a living testimony of hate. She was aware she had to forgive him because he was dead. But she wasted years hating him instead of forgiving him and finding someone else to love, someone who would love her the right way.

God requires us to forgive those who hurt us. She made a choice to live with an unforgiving heart. She spent years alone, without the joy of love in her life. I felt sorry for her. I learned that day to let my anger and hate go, because it can ruin your life.

#LessonLearned

PAY ATTENTION

Our Reminder Text –

But seek first his kingdom and his righteousness, and all these things will be given to you as well.

Matthew 6:33 NIV

Marvin Sapp has a song called "Praise Him in Advance". Initially when the song came out, I didn't understand the lyrics, or perhaps I should say I didn't want to accept them. When the song came out I was in the process of getting a divorce, and I was angry. I recall thinking, how do you praise Him in advance when you do not know how He is going to work it out? I was perplexed about how I was going to sell my business, provide for my daughters and create a future for myself. I was experiencing so many emotions at once, and I remember asking God, "Why would you allow me to experience this?"

I'll explain the why on another day.

Now I'm pretty certain this is what most of us believers call going through a storm. My storm was overwhelming me because I'd become consumed with solving my own problems. I was over-whelmed because I was trying to solve my problems instead of allowing God to solve them for me. Most of the time many of us struggle with the solution, but I believe God wants us to learn from the process, and not only the result.

As we live, we should grow from every experience. God wants to take our relationship with Him even deeper. When is the last time you wore your pants out praying on your knees? Have you done an all-night prayer meeting? For most of us, the answers to these questions are I don't remember and No! To get extraordinary power we must go deeper in Christ. Today, commit yourself to going deeper in Christ. The solution shouldn't be your only focus. The process is important too. Pay attention to the process. I finally did.

#LessonLearned

TIME WELL SPENT

Our Reminder Text –

**Do not boast about tomorrow,
For you do not know what a day may bring forth.**

Proverbs 27:1 KJV

Recently, my stepdaughter Traci called, and during our conversation she mentioned that a friend of their family had lost their twenty-something year old daughter in a car accident. I was sad to hear that any parent had to bury their child, but it got me to thinking. When we lose a young person it always seems to affect me differently than an older person. Why is that? I think we see their life cut short as a disservice. We wonder why God would allow them to die at such a young age.

Over the years I have lost friends and asked God why? A few years ago, after a young man in my church suddenly died, I started asking God "Why am I still here?". For a long time, I didn't get any answers. Then one day I was on breakfast duty in my school. I noticed a young lady, who for some reason, came to school every day wearing clothes that were way too tight. Well, I finally asked her why her clothes did not fit her.

She said, "This is all my momma gave me".

I asked her, what size she wore, she didn't know. At the time, I wore a 16 and she was bigger, so I guessed she had to wear an 18.

We checked her jeans they were a size 12, the shirt was too small too, it was a medium. I left work and headed to Walmart to buy some clothes. I explained to the manager what I needed. He offered me a gift card. With my donated funds and the gift card, I was able to buy her some clothes, undergarments and a pair of shoes. On my way back to school I heard a voice say, "There is still work for you to do". There was my answer. The rest of the week I thanked God for answering my prayer. I still had work to do.

Just because a life is cut short does not mean their life didn't have purpose. The days we are given are precious. I learned a young life still has purpose. They loved, they shared, and they mattered. And they made an impact. Youthfulness has nothing to do with living out our purpose. I still have work to do. And if you're reading this today so do you. Use your time wisely. Ask God" Why am I still here?"

#LessonLearned

HURRICANE LESSONS

Our Reminder Text –

You will keep in perfect peace those whose minds are steadfast, because they trust in you.

Isaiah 26:3 NIV

My hurricane experience taught me a few lessons. My neighborhood sits up against a levee which is fed from a local river. As the rain saturated our city the levee started to fill up.

On a Monday evening, the local sheriff and police officers came to talk to our neighborhood about evacuating. They shared information about the levee, and how they felt with the continued rain it would break and flood our subdivision. They insisted on a mandatory evacuation for the homes in the rear of my subdivision. As we listened to them explain the details, I looked around the room at the angry faces of my neighbors.

After the sheriff explained either they leave or don't call them if and when the levee breaks. Many of my neighbors were upset. They didn't want to leave their homes and definitely didn't appreciate the tone of the officials.

The next day, as we left to volunteer the police came back and shut down power to those homes which might be in danger. They were forced to leave.

While I know that this was inconvenient, I do understand that this was for their protection. Here is what's interesting, many of us are just like my neighbors. God has given us His love and yet many of us refuse to take it. He has given us warnings, and yet we ignore those warnings.

The Bible clearly has given us example after example of people who went against God's word. Yet, we ignore that still small voice, and forge full speed ahead in the wrong direction.

The blessing, I believe, is that I had everybody I know praying that water away. God protected my neighborhood. To this day, not one drop of water has come out of that levee. That's due to the power of prayer.

I hope my neighbors learned a lesson, I know I did.

#LessonLearned

A LESSON IN FAILURE

Our Reminder Text –

Therefore, since we are surrounded by such a great cloud of witnesses, let us throw off everything that hinders and the sin that so easily entangles. And let us run with perseverance the race marked out for us, fixing our eyes on Jesus, the pioneer and perfecter of faith. For the joy set before him he endured the cross, scorning its shame, and sat down at the right hand of the throne of God. Consider him who endured such opposition from sinners, so that you will not grow weary and lose heart.

Hebrews 12:1-3 NIV

The word perseverance is defined as "steady persistence in a course of action, a purpose, a state, especially in spite of difficulties, obstacles, or discouragement." Perseverance is a choice. Each day, we make decisions to move forward.

A few years ago, I had to take a state exam. I will be the first to admit that I am not a great test taker. I usually get test anxiety and forget everything. And just as I had in previous years, I got into the testing room and forgot everything I studied. I failed the test. I was heartbroken, I had to pass the test that year in order to get my teacher's certification. I knew when I left the room that I had failed. I told my husband and he comforted me, suggesting to me that next time I pray about my test, continue to study, and figure out a way to keep myself calm during the test.

For a month, I studied and waited to register for the test again, and that test date came fast. This time, I decided not to stress over the test; I decided to create a studying system. I studied every day for three months, only breaking on the weekends.

I created a way to calm my nerves – I prayed. I systematically started to pray before and after I studied.

On my test day, I walked into the room at ease and took the test. After seven days, my results came, and I passed! Now, I could have given up, but I am not a person who gives up easily. I knew that God allowed me to fail the test because I hadn't trusted in Him as I was studying. My decision to create a prayer circle around my test is what I believe made the difference.

I persevered in studying for this exam despite my dyslexia. I offered my disability to God and asked Him to help me overcome this challenge, and He answered my prayer. I share this to help other people realize that, with God's help, all things are possible. With God's help, I have overcome many of life's challenges, and there is nothing I can't overcome with His help.

#LessonLearned

LESSONS IN THE CLASSROOM

Our Reminder Text –

But the Lord said unto Samuel, look not on his countenance, or on the height of his stature; because I have refused him: for the Lord seeth not as man seeth; for man looketh on the outward appearance, but the Lord looketh on the heart.

1 Samuel 16:7 KJV

The beginning of a new year is always exciting. I look forward to seeing all of the new faces that I will be stuck with for 180 days. I am just joking – I love my students.

This year, I have five classes and was excited to meet my new students. On the first day of school, a male African-American student walked into my class and he gave off a foul odor as he passed me. I wasn't sure what the smell was, but it wasn't good.

I have a tradition at the beginning of the year to explain the rules of engagement in my classroom. In my speech, I give them the do's and don'ts, I fully explain my expectations and what will make me go over the edge. It's really quite comical; I've been doing this stand-up for years.

During my speech, I noticed the same young man had fallen asleep. *I know I am not that boring that he would be falling asleep already. It's day one,* I thought to myself. *How can he be falling asleep this early in the day?* I overlooked it, kept talking, eased my way over to him, and called his name to wake him up.

On the second day, this same young man fell asleep in my class again. Again, I walked over and called his name. He was knocked out. This time, I tapped him on the shoulder. He didn't budge a bit. He didn't hear me calling his name. I let him sleep for about 20 minutes. Once the bell rang, I walked over and woke him up. I didn't ask why he was so sleepy; I just assumed he was tired from getting back into the routine of school.

On days three and four he fell asleep again. Now I was beginning to think he must be up half the night playing video games, that's got to be it. I had determined in my mind to speak to him about his video game parties and insist he go to bed at an earlier time. On day five, he fell asleep almost five minutes into class. When the classroom lights came back on after watching a video clip, he was completely asleep. Now I was annoyed. Not only was he falling asleep when I talked, but he fell asleep on the lesson's support video.

When he woke up, I asked to speak to him after class. I had my speech ready about the reasons why he needed to go to bed early and stop partying or playing video games at night. When I asked why he was always falling asleep in my class, his response was,

"Mrs. Blackwell, I am so sorry, but I've been getting home from my second job late, so I am really struggling to stay awake during the day."

My spirit hit the floor. I said, "Son, did you say your second job? How many jobs do you have?"

"I work two jobs and go to school," he said. "My mom needs help paying the bills, so I got to work!"

I had no response. I encouraged him to try to talk to his supervisor, so he can get off early.

My student was exhausted. I felt really bad for assuming he was goofing off, when instead he was working; and unlike most people his age, he was working very hard to support his mother and brother. Now, I let him sleep for a few minutes and give him time to clean up, so he can focus on school.

The Bible says that "man looketh on the outward appearance, but the Lord looketh at the heart" (1 Samuel 16:7 KJV). I've learned not to assume the worst of people. In my line of work, I am used to students lying, and even parents lying or being hostile when I call about their child. It's a genuine surprise when a student is truthful and struggling like this young man. He is trying to stay awake, and I try to allow him some rest time on days he is tired. I was taught to never judge a book by its cover.

#LessonLearned

PAULA BLACKWELL

LESSONS IN THE TURBULENCE

Our Reminder Text –

"Wait on the Lord: be of good courage, and he shall strengthen thine heart: wait, I say, on the Lord"

Psalm 27:14 KJV

As an author and speaker, I travel pretty frequently. I am very thankful and don't take for granted that each time I board a plane, it is a miracle that it lands safely.

What is unnerving to most people is turbulence. I don't like it either, but after years of flying, I recognize that not every flight will go as smoothly as I would like. There will be days when you will experience turbulence.

Have you prayed about a situation in your life and found yourself waiting for a breakthrough? Are you wondering why the answer hasn't come yet? Do you feel as though victory is passing you by?

Sometimes, when we pray long and hard about a situation in our life without receiving any answers, we just learn to live with it. We go on about our business, wondering if, or when God will send the answer. But God does hear those prayers, and He's working out the answers even though we may not know all of the details. Our situation can change suddenly — quickly without warning!

Turbulence is a fact of life. Not every day will be sunny; there will sometimes be some rain. The key is how you weather the turbulence. Will you give up? Will you ask God for help? Will you submit to His will? Or will you stand still and watch God deliver you? There are times when we try to fix the turbulence in our lives ourselves. I can attest, that has never worked out for me.

I recall trying to fix a situation and I ended up not fixing it, and in fact, making it worse. It was at that moment that I realized I needed to allow God to fix the situation.

By the time I realized what I had done, I had to ask God to fix an even bigger problem. Asking God after I made a complete disaster was not the right decision. The only way this works is by trusting God.

I learned the hard way to wait on God. There is a rap song my students used to sing a few years ago that went, "If I move you move." Well, if God tells me to move, I move. If He doesn't say anything, then I stand still. Waiting on God isn't always easy, but it's necessary.

#LessonLearned

#REFILL

#REFILL

I wish my car could run forever and the gas tank never go empty. That would save me a lot of money. But as we Journey, one of the Lessons we realize is that everything and everyone needs to be ReFilled. In this section we explore our need to be refreshed and God's promises of lavish replenishing. At the end of each day in this section there is a challenge to help you apply the lessons you are learning.

> *"'In the last days, God says, I will pour out my Spirit on all people..."*
>
> *Acts 2:17*
>
> *Kymone Hinds*

 @kymonehinds

BROKEN SENSORS

To put off your old self, which belongs to your former manner of life and is corrupt through deceitful desires, and to be renewed in the spirit of your minds, and to put on the new self, created after the likeness of God in true righteousness and holiness.

Ephesians 4:22-24 ESV

If you have ever driven a car, or paid attention while a passenger, you have seen it. It's that irritating light on the panel in front of the steering wheel. It stays on while you drive, and everything may seem fine except the light won't go off.

If you are like me, you have ignored that light from time to time. If it did not say gas or oil, you kept on driving because maybe nothing was wrong, or if it was something, it was no big deal. A check engine light can easily become common if we ignore it long enough.

I think I have developed the ability to ignore it because I have seen it on before and investigated it and found out that nothing was in fact wrong with my car. The light was on as a false warning because of a broken sensor. The assumption I have developed is that when the light goes on there is something wrong with a sensor, not the engine.

But as we think about it, it is so much more dangerous when the sensor is broken, and it doesn't give any reading at all when something is drastically wrong. When our engine is about to over-heat, and no light comes on, that's the real danger. And that is the danger that you and I live with every day.

In Ephesians 4, the writer Paul is describing what the Christian walk should look like. He talks about unity and now in the latter verses he talks about what belongs and what doesn't belong to the life of a believer. He uses this phrase that is interesting to me - "your old self....is corrupt through deceitful desires." (Emphasis added).

There is a sense here that we are in danger of following something that we deem to be trustworthy but can actually mislead us. We can be led into sensuality, greed, indifference, and drifting away from God because of something as natural as our desires - because of what we feel like doing. Desires are natural to us. We all have them. But this verse warns us that our desires can be deceitful. They can lead us to want things that are not for our good and against God's will for us.

If all we were left to were our feelings, we would be led astray. If all we had to make decisions about what is right and wrong, were our cravings, we would be off. Our sensor is broken so that it doesn't always tell us when there is danger. We may not see anything wrong with something because we "want it," but that is because our desires are misleading at times. Our sensor is broken.

The good news for us all is that God has sent His Holy Spirit for this exact reason. He is to convict us of what is right, show us what is wrong and give us the power of discernment. God has given us a new sensor. God's Spirit is to act as a means of pointing out to us danger. He is sent to override our desires that may tell us wrong is right and right is wrong, and He gives us a true perspective on life.

What we are called to do is to trust the leading of God's Spirit. Don't lean on our own understanding. In all our ways, acknowledge Him, seek His leading. And He will direct our path. Let's be honest enough to admit that our feelings aren't always right and humble enough to seek the leading of the Holy Spirit to guide us.

Challenge for the Day:

One thing that stops our spiritual growth is ignoring the presence of sin in our lives. It chokes out room for God's Spirit. Spend some time examining yourself this week. Confess the sins that God has been giving you conviction about. Ask Him for the power to overcome. Take necessary next steps to walk in the victory He has given you.

HE'S IN YOU

Therefore, my beloved, as you have always obeyed, so now, not only as in my presence but much more in my absence, work out your own salvation with fear and trembling, for it is God who works in you, both to will and to work for his good pleasure.

Philippians 2:12-13 ESV

"Is it in you?" That's the slogan for the sports energy drink Gatorade. Growing up I remember thinking if I ever drink some Gatorade, I too could "be like Mike." (Michael Jordan for all young people reading this). Well that didn't happen obviously, but I have since learned to appreciate another Gatorade product other than the drink.

I was running with some friends, and one of them offered me some goo. It's a thick paste that comes in a pack you squeeze into your mouth. At first, I was skeptical. But after you have run for so long and you are exhausted, you will try almost anything. So, I took some Gatorade goo. It worked! It gave me an energy boost. It was in me. It powered me to run faster and further.

Paul gives a challenge in Philippians 2. He is writing to a church he had organized in Philippi. They are people he had won to Christ and helped to grow in Christ. And now he is separated from them. He is telling them to stay consistent even though he's not around. He tells them to "work out your own salvation with fear and trembling."

He is telling them to not be dependent on his presence to live the way they know how to live. It's their salvation and they can work it out, even without their spiritual leader being there. He is saying you have it - salvation. Now use it. Just like them, we don't have to work for our salvation, but we are called to exercise it - let the fact we are saved affect the way we live.

Then Paul adds something that gives us encouragement today:

> *"For it is God who works in you, both to will and to work for his good pleasure."* Phil. 2:13

After telling them to exercise the salvation experience, he assures them that they have the ultimate energy boost. God is working inside of them and inside of us. Because God knows we get tired and lose motivation, He comes in us to give us the desire and then works through us. He powers us to want and to work.

What a God we serve! He doesn't just save us. He then comes inside of us and works at the level of desire...He helps us to want to live out our salvation. There are times you and I lose motivation to serve God. God assures us, I am working in you all along and especially at those times, to cause you to want to serve me.

Then after God has given us the desire to do what He wants us to, He gives the strength to do it. God initiates saving us. Then calls us to live it out. But He enables us to do what He has called us to do. Are you lacking motivation, desire, strength, power? Ask God to give you the boost of the power of His Spirit – He will. Are you weak and unable to keep promises? Ask God to give you the power of His Spirit. He's in you.

Challenge for the Day:

Do something different to add variety to your devotional time. If you are accustomed to praying on your knees, try a prayer walk. If you only read and pray in your time with God, add music and singing. Do something different.

MAY I HAVE ANOTHER?

**The steadfast love of the Lord never ceases;
his mercies never come to an end;
they are new every morning;
great is your faithfulness.**

Lamentations 3:22-23 ESV

My children love going to the bank. There are two problems with that statement I just made that can get me in trouble. The first is, you may assume we have a lot of money in the bank and that is why they like to go. That's not the case, and that's not why they like going to the bank.

They don't care about what transaction I was going to the drive through at the bank to conduct. They are only there for the lollipops. If you are a dentist or dietician, I just got in trouble with you. Even if we are doing an ATM transaction, they will ask me to drive back around to go through the teller line to ask for the candy.

I don't know if my children have ever thought about it, but I have. I have wondered how many bags of lollipops they have back there. I have wondered if there ever comes a time when some parent with young ones like mine will eventually drive through and ask and they say to them "we gave out the last one just before you came." Or maybe one day the same teller at the same drive through, would eventually say to a repeater like me "that's it - no more lollipops for you...you came yesterday for some."

I highly doubt any of my scenarios above would ever occur. Something tells me that there is a company policy or at least an unwritten rule that you always keep the candy supply stocked and replenish often, because people will ask for it. And I can't help but think that even more than that, God's bank in heaven keeps a fresh supply of mercy because people like you and me will need it.

In the passage above, the writer is a prophet by the name of Jeremiah. He is living in a very difficult time and his book is called Lamentations for a good reason; it's like an extended blues song. It tells of the troubles people are going through. But then he inserts these verses that tell why he has hope in the midst of the difficulties. "(God's) mercies never come to an end."

That's good news for us. That's great news for us! We need God's mercies more than children desire candy. The Bible lets us know that God never runs out, and He actually refills the supply each day - "they are new every morning."

My challenge and your challenge, is believing that. Many times, we drift, wander away and stay away from God because we think that asking for mercy again will get us some of the responses from above. We think God will say "there's no more left" or "you received some already today, you can't have anymore." But that's not the God we serve. His supply is limitless, and He is more willing to extend it to us than we are willing to ask.

As we seek to grow in our daily walk with God and with spending time with Him, we will mess up along the way. That's inevitable. When we do, we are tempted to beat ourselves up and even want to quit. But I encourage you come back to the bank of heaven…. there's more mercy available for our sins.

Someone at my local bank must be going out and purchasing these lollipops. They are not showing up in the teller's area all by themselves. Someone has to pay for what my kids get for free. Someone has paid for the mercy of God. It didn't show up by itself. We get it for free because Jesus paid for it by giving His life on the cross. The supply is unending, it is refilled each day and it is yours...just ask for it.

Challenge for the Day:

This week make a playlist for your worship time. Identify songs that draw your heart closer to God. They can be hymns you sing, songs you listen to on a device, or instrumentals you play. Use them for your worship time each day this week. Let music bring you into God's presence today.

THAT'S SAYING A HEART FULL

The good person out of the good treasure of his heart produces good, and the evil person out of his evil treasure produces evil, for out of the abundance of the heart his mouth speaks.

Luke 6:45 ESV

My mouth is filled with your praise,
and with your glory all the day.

Psalm 71:8 ESV

One day I walked into my bathroom and the floor was flooded with water. It was everywhere. Carpets were wet, and the floor was slippery. I immediately began attacking the water on the floor by finding pieces of clothing to dry it up. But it didn't take me long to realize that it was a futile endeavor. I didn't just need to attack the water on the floor, I had to stop the cause of the flood.

Someone, (I think one of my adorable children in their younger years) had left the faucet running, and they also had dropped something in the sink to impede the flow of water down the drain. The water in the sink spilled onto the floor.

There are times when it seems you and I have a lot to say. You can't help yourself. It just spills out of you and you don't know where all of what you said came from. You didn't plan to say what you said. You didn't plan to share as much as you shared. You didn't plan to reveal as much as you revealed but after you're finished someone may say to you, "you just said a mouthful." You didn't plan to say it all, but it was in your heart.

There is a connection to what you say and what is in your heart. What we talk about, discuss, and share, is connected to what we think about, contemplate and care deeply about. Jesus said in Luke 6:45 that *"out of the abundance of the heart, his mouth speaks."*

Jesus is saying that many times, we see the effects of things and begin attacking the spills and drying it up, but there is a deeper issue involved. Sometimes we are dismayed by what we say and want to "bite our tongue" but the root of the issue is what is in our heart. For whatever is in our heart will spill out in what we say. We not only say a "mouthful", we say a "heart full."

So, what is the solution for people like you and me who struggle with the things we say? What do we do when we have issues with gossip, negative talk, lying and more? Well there are a couple of things we can do to help fill our hearts with the right things.

First, we can spend time contemplating God and His goodness to us. All of us have more blessings that we have received than we take the time to regularly acknowledge. God has done things for us, for our salvation, that we need to spend more time meditating about. In addition, God is day by day showing tangible evidence of His personal care for us. Let's fill our hearts by spending time reflecting on the goodness of God.

The second way I want to encourage us to fill our hearts with positive things is to talk more about God and His goodness. You may be thinking, isn't that the opposite of what was said before? Didn't we say we need a full heart to have our mouth say the right things? Well it actually is a cycle. What is in the heart comes out of the mouth. But also, what comes out of the mouth affects the heart.

So, if you want your heart to be full of the things of God, fill your mouth with the praise of God. Over and over, it is modeled and commanded to fill our mouth with thanksgiving, prayer, and praise to God. It lifts our hearts, and as we do, fills our hearts and then comes out in even more thanks from our lips to God.

This week, you will say many things to many people. You will share about life's challenges, life's successes, and different things on your heart. What if this week when we share with people, we are so filled with the goodness of God, that they can hear that coming through everything we say? That's saying a heart full.

Challenge for the Day:

Spend some time at the beginning of each day writing out a list of at least 10 things you are thankful for. Try and write a different list each day. Spend time contemplating the list each day. As you talk during the day, seek opportunity to share the goodness of God from that list with someone.

TIRED OF LEFTOVERS

And Moses said to them, "Let no one leave any of it over till the morning." But they did not listen to Moses. Some left part of it till the morning, and it bred worms and stank. And Moses was angry with them...

Exodus 16:19-20 ESV

Give us this day our daily bread.

Matthew 6:11 ESV

Last week was one of the best celebrations I have ever had in my life. Family and dear friends came to town. Multiple surprise gatherings were planned for me. There were thoughtful and kind gestures extended to me that were so overwhelming. Turning 40 was great.One of the residual blessings after the weekend was an abundance of food - great food. We had to make room in our refrigerator for all that we received. I was incredibly grateful. But I was reminded about a fact of life. There is such a thing as too much of the same thing.

After day number 3 you may not be as enthusiastic to eat the same leftovers, no matter how good they were. There comes a time when you need something fresh. That goes not only for physical food, but spiritual food as well.

In the account of the Exodus of the Israelites from Egypt, God told Moses that He would rain bread from heaven. You could not get a better chef than God, so the food provided had to be just heavenly (pun intended). The Israelites were able to get as much, or as little as they could eat that day. However, there was an important caution. This food was good for one day only.

Maybe there is a lesson for us all in our spiritual life. There are times we receive such a spiritual boost from a sermon, a Bible teaching, a time of devotion, a worship experience or a song. We feel like we can live off of that for a while. That is a real temptation - to live today on yesterday's bread.

God has a fresh supply of grace and mercy for us each day. He also has a fresh provision of spiritual nourishment for us each day as we spend time with Him in His word and in prayer. What God has to feed our soul each day is just what we need to meet the challenges of the day ahead.

It is amazing that God has everything we need for life, but He gives it to us in daily provision. He wants us to depend on Him and come back to Him for our supply each day. So, this week my challenge to us all is to not live off of leftovers.

Make your time with God each day sacred, and guard it carefully. It is vital to your spiritual help. Get some fresh bread.

Challenge for the Day:
_____

Spend more time today writing out a list of at least 10 things you are thankful for. Try and write a different list each day. Spend time contemplating the list each day. As you talk during the day, seek opportunity to share the goodness of God from that list with someone.

WHAT DO YOU HAVE?

_____

"Then Peter said, "Silver and gold I do not have, but what I do have I give you: In the name of Jesus Christ of Nazareth, rise up and walk." And he took him by the right hand and lifted him up, and immediately his feet and ankle bones received strength."

Acts 3:6-7 NKJV

_____

A few years ago, I took my wife to Trinidad for the first time. I love the island that I grew up on and was so excited to show her around and have her experience a taste of my upbringing. One day I took her out sight-seeing. We had a great time, but after a while we got hungry.

We were excited to find a local food shop that advertised various island delicacies. Just reading their menu made our mouths water. We placed an order and one of the people in the front went in the back and came back to report "we don't have that." We inquired about a few other items on the menu and received the same reply - "we don't have that."

After going through that a couple more times my wife finally asked a better question - "what do you have?"

It can be frustrating when we list in our lives all the things we do not have. When we can list our deficiencies, our shortcomings, our deficits. Truth is, we are quite good at that. We can list all the things we do not have in order to do what life asks us to do.

In the Biblical narrative found in Acts 3:1-10, we find Peter and John meeting a situation that exposed their lack. They are approached by a lame beggar as they are going for a prayer service at the temple. He asks them for money and Peter's response is classic. "Look at us," he tells the man. In other words, do we look like we have any money?

What Peter says next is what is instructive to all of us. He says, "Silver and gold I do not have, but what I do have I give you." Peter did not have money. He was empty in that area. But earlier in Acts we found out they were filled with the Holy Spirit. And because Peter and John were filled with the Spirit, instead of giving spare change, they offered life change.

Each of us is lacking something in life. Maybe money, space, time, knowledge. Even as a church family we have definite areas we can declare 'we don't have.' However, our focus this year as individuals and as a church family should be on being filled with the Spirit of God.

So, when we encounter situations and circumstances in life that call for action, we can answer the question "what do you have," with the answer "we are filled with the Spirit of God." The Spirit of God is available to us today. Let us spend time with God so we can be filled with His Spirit.

Challenge for the Day:

_____

Get a prayer journal. It can be a simple notebook. Use it in your prayer time. You can write out your prayer to God. Promises you are claiming and even challenging things you are experiencing in life. Keep a record of your time with God.

TRUST THE PROCESS

And I am sure of this, that he who began a good work in you will bring it to completion at the day of Jesus Christ.

Philippians 1:6 ESV

It seems like road construction follows us where we live. We lived in Kansas City for 7 years and there was always a highway being worked on at some point. When we moved to Memphis in 2012, it seemed like the crews, the signs, and the hassle of roadwork tagged along.

Our commute to the Overton Park Church building, or to the Alcy SDA Jr Academy where our children attended school, involved driving down Highway 40. It was congested enough when we arrived in 2012, but that got so much worse when they decided to do an expansion of the highway. There would be times when the multi-lane roadway would turn into a parking lot.

There was a sign on it saying when the work would be completed. That never seemed to give me comfort while sitting in my car waiting for movement. The date seemed so far away. Until one day it happened - construction was finished and my commute time had been cut by at least 7 minutes from the pre-construction time (I can get up to 10 minutes faster...but you shouldn't try that). The wait and inconvenience has been worth it. I needed to trust the process.

Truth is, none of us like processes. We like instantaneous fixes. But God specializes in processes. In fact, while you read this devotion, you are a work in process. There is a construction crew working in you. And there is even a future date of completion.

The Bible says in Philippians 1:6, "He who began a good work in you..." God is working in you.

I don't know about you, but that's one of those good-bad news statements. It means that the Person who is working on my character and shaping and molding me is God, and He can be trusted. The difficult part is that construction is never convenient. It involves shifting things out of place, we don't always see the immediate benefit and sometimes we are tempted to want to call a halt to the whole thing. Those are the times we need to trust the process.

Ultimately, I am glad that God takes responsibility for the work on the inside of us. We know we can't fix up ourselves no matter how hard we try on our own. The news gets even better. There is a completion date for this construction job.

"He who began a good work in you will bring it to completion at the day of Jesus Christ."

There is coming a day when we will see the full effects of God's work in us, when Jesus comes. I know we will all agree that all the discomfort, inconvenience, challenges, they will all be worth it. Trust the process.

Challenge for the Day:
_____

Look up Bible verses about "Christ in you." Look at the work He promised to do in you. Thank Him for that work even now.

#ME, MY SELFIE & I AM

#ME, MY SELFIE + I AM

Hey! Hey! Hey! You have just entered a different section of your reading called Me, My Selfie & I AM! This section is about time with God. Let's take a journey with God, Biblical characters and some testimonies from the Word of God. I pray that you will encounter God in a new way and see how you fit in to His large universal plan! Take a Selfie with God and put Him in the picture of your life each day. Claim His promises and follow His directions!

**And you will seek Me and find Me,
when you search for Me with all your heart.**

Jeremiah 29:13

Philip M. Wesley II

McGuire Entertainment Group

@pastorphil2

ME, MY SELFIE + I AM

_____

**And you will seek Me and find Me,
when you search for Me with all your heart.**

Jeremiah 29:13 NKJV

_____

Throughout the Bible there are amazing characters that have experienced the same matters we encounter today. They have experienced heartbreaks and heartaches, failures and victories, and all throughout their stories we see how phenomenal God is through the process of learning.

Me, My Selfie, and I AM is all about time with God. Let's take a journey with God through these characters and some testimonies from the Word of God. I pray that you will encounter God in a new way and see how you fit into His large universal plan! Take a Selfie with God and put Him in the picture of your life each day. Claim His promises and follow His directions!

WORDS WITH FRIENDS

Death and life are in the power of the tongue,
And those who love it will eat its fruit.

Proverbs 18:21 NKJV

I love playing Words with Friends. This game is an electronic way to play scrabble. My first scrabble game was on a Palm Pilot (it's an old version of an Electronic Organizer, Google that one), If you are a regular on this game, you may have 10 or more games going at the same time. I find that it relaxes me and helps me think critically. As I was playing today, I began to reflect on life.

The object of the game is to beat your opponent at forming words. Players take turns forming words on the board, or they may choose to swap tiles with the pool of currently unused tiles or pass their turn. You can form words either vertically or horizontally on the board.

The aim is to score as many points as possible. Scores can be doubled if a word is placed on the Double Word space. The word will have a triple value if it is placed on the Triple word space. But in the end whoever has the most points wins.

Whether you are in conversation with a friend, spouse, public speaking, writing, they all have the same theory. The right words in the right place can take you a long way! There is power in the words that we speak, we can use it to encourage or discourage. The right words can be used to clear up a misconception. As a parent, we teach our kids how to use their words rather than point at objects or people. Words are used to describe how we are feeling, speak our desires or argue our point. Words can make or break someone's day.

I've learned that Words are powerful, and with Friends they are more valuable when they are used to obtain the best results. God's word teaches us that the power of life is in the tongue.

Can you remember a time that you used the wrong words in the right space?

WHY DOES GOD ALLOW TROUBLE?

"We are troubled on every side, yet not distressed; we are perplexed, but not in despair; Persecuted, but not forsaken; cast down, but not destroyed;"

2 Corinthians 4:8 KJV

"I'm vexed, fumed, I had it up to here" a classic line by the late Phife Dawg in A Tribe Called Quest's Scenario recording. Over the span of my 42 years, I've had my share of aggravations and it all comes down to expectations of life. Pastor Andy Stanley once related that, unrealistic expectations lead to great disappointments. What we expect out of people, or life itself, can determine our peace, or frustrations. I have learned that if we expect not to have trouble then we are in trouble! In speaking with people whether they are Christian or atheist, it comes down to this same false expectation of God that there should be no troubles in life. I've often heard If there is a God why does He allow so much pain and suffering when He can easily stop it? Why is the #MeToo story growing by the day? Why is there human trafficking? Why is there slavery in Africa? Why is racism still a major topic of discussion? What is going on in this world? When will God put an end to this? We talk about Jesus coming soon, but it doesn't seem to be soon enough! What is God doing on His fancy throne, in His perfect world in the sky?

I do have the answer, and I'm not sure you will like it. Remember that small tree in the Garden of Eden that God told us not to eat from? Remember He told us the moment we eat from that tree is the moment we will die? Oh, you thought it was limited to Adam and Eve? When will we take full responsibility for our actions? When will we stop blaming God and start thanking Him for not making matters worse? We chose this life of pain and suffering, however, here is the good news.... God had a backup plan to get us through all trouble! He promised we would have trouble, yet we will not be destroyed! He promised that He will fix all of this one day and there will be no more death or sorrow even though we chose this, we have a better solution. We can choose to be free and live forever. God sent His son to die and kill death so that we can live! I promise you this today, stay with God and trouble won't last always!

TRUST AGAIN

**Even my own familiar friend in whom I trusted,
Who ate my bread, Has lifted up his heel against me.**

Psalm 41:9 NKJV

Have you ever been hurt by someone close to you? I mean betrayed by someone you considered a best friend or even spouse? How do you deal with such betrayal? Was that relationship over? Were you able to restore it? Were you able to trust again?

Trust is the mecca of all relationships. If there is no trust, there is no real relationship. Trust is a risk-taking adventure that everyone must take. What happens if we trust the first time and get hurt? The next person to enter into the equation will have a tough time earning our trust. Therefore, we resort to being wall engineers. We build walls to protect us from getting hurt again.

What is the worst thing that can happen?

Think about it. What if you get hurt again? How many times of getting hurt is enough? Then I beg to question, if you are a person that is getting hurt the same way over and over, is it really the wall you need to build for the next person? Have you looked deep inside yourself to see what you need to adjust? Why do you end up in the same type of relationships? Have you really figured out yourself? I know there are a lot of questions, however, it is necessary to address the inner person.

I had to talk to me.

After several relationships that didn't work out, I had to take a look deep inside to see what was wrong. I stopped blaming me, or the other person. I have learned that two great people aren't so great together. That is across the board in relationships. In my experience, if you haven't learned to forgive, you can't learn to trust. Trust doesn't mean you go back to the same place, it means we learn to evaluate ourselves and the people that enter our happy space. Trust your gut, if something isn't right, God may be speaking to you. First, trust God! God will lead you in the right path. Trust isn't easy; however, we can trust again…. it's necessary!

THE GAME OF GODS

**Then the serpent said to the woman,
"You will not surely die. For God knows that
in the day you eat of it your eyes will be opened,
and you will be like God, knowing good and evil."**

Genesis 3: 4-5 NKJV

"Happy wife, happy life!" Nothing further from the truth! The fact that we are making one partner's needs more important than the other is an epic fail for a relationship. Healthy relationships are not about who has more divinity than the other. There is a fine line between being desired and being worshipped. There is no doubt we as humans should feel loved, desired and appreciated, however, if ones needs become dominant over the other, chances are it is not a healthy relationship, and one is just staying quiet to keep the peace.

Adam and Eve set us up for this epidemic. They were as close to gods as a human could get. Perfect world, spouse, and leader. The serpent convinced Eve that God was just holding everyone back from divinity. While they already had true happiness, they allowed another broken relationship to sabotage their peace of mind. Since then, man has tried to dominate each other through abuse, slavery, manipulation, and false worship. We have learned how to get people to do what we want for all the wrong reasons, and still haven't found true joy. Why? We are playing the game of gods. Can you really handle the power you desire? God can, humans are shaky! In Ancient Rome, the Auriga was a slave with gladiator status, whose duty was to drive a chariot, and was carefully selected among trustworthy slaves only. As the military commander would parade through town receiving praise for his victory, Auriga would whisper in his ears Memento homo (remember you are (only) a man), to avoid the excess of celebration that could lead the celebrated commander to lose his sense of proportions. My advice to you today is to treat each other with love, respect, and honor, just remember you're only human!

PRAY AND DON'T GIVE UP

One day Jesus told his disciples a story to show that they should always pray and never give up. "There was a judge in a certain city," he said, "who neither feared God nor cared about people. A widow of that city came to him repeatedly, saying, 'Give me justice in this dispute with my enemy.' The judge ignored her for a while, but finally he said to himself, 'I don't fear God or care about people, but this woman is driving me crazy. I'm going to see that she gets justice, because she is wearing me out with her constant requests!'" Then the Lord said, "Learn a lesson from this unjust judge. Even he rendered a just decision in the end. So, don't you think God will surely give justice to his chosen people who cry out to him day and night? Will he keep putting them off? I tell you, he will grant justice to them quickly! But when the Son of Man returns, how many will he find on the earth who have faith?"

Luke 18:1-8 NKJV

This is one of my favorite stories in the Bible. I had to share in its entirety. Justice is what this world is calling for today. Sexual abusers beware, liars, cheaters, murderers and thieves are put on notice now. The oppressed are crying out and God is answering. Some may still be wondering if God will help the oppressed. God speaks clearly in this story about a woman that wanted to settle matters with her enemy. She was consistent in calling on the judge to solve the problem rather than doing it herself. Jesus says learn a lesson from the unjust judge, who didn't care about God or people, yet he still gave justice. Pray and never give up on the just God. Be bold about what you need from God.

Do you need justice in your relationship, finances, health, living arrangements, or your job? Maybe all of the above? God loves us, and He cares. I'm learning to be courageous in my requests to God. I am learning to know and ask for what I want and need. I know God is listening, and He's ready to answer. Pray and don't give up!

MY HEART

"The human heart is the most deceitful of all things, and desperately wicked. Who really knows how bad it is?

Jeremiah 17:2 NKJV

God knows my heart! Have you ever heard that in a conversation with someone who feels condemned by another? They usually say it, so no one would judge them. And you know what? I agree! God looks at the heart while men pay attention to the exterior. However, consider the fact that the human heart is deceitful. David consistently asked God to examine his heart to see if there were any wicked ways in him. Testing of the heart will prove if the heart is seeking God or seeking one's own desires. So before saying God knows my heart, ask God to examine your heart.

God can give us a clean heart and pull us closer to Him. Indeed, God does know our heart; But that doesn't give us license to stay the way we are. By being in the presence of God our lives should change. Don't just say it, ask God to examine and fix it. The heart is deceitful. It tells us we are doing ok when we are really in a horrible state. It tells us we are in love when maybe we are blinded by lust or some other irrational desires. The heart makes us stay places we should clearly leave, trust people we should run a background check on, and it tells us we are safe when we have tons of insecurities!

Trust God with your heart and He will never lead you down the path of destruction! Use divine wisdom in all things! Trust your instincts and trust the Spirit. Let God know your heart, and give you a new one. God does know our hearts! **"But I, the Lord, search all hearts and examine secret motives. I give all people their due rewards, according to what their actions deserve." Jeremiah 17:10 NLT**

I HAVE A PACKAGE FOR YOU!

"For the wages of sin is death, but the free gift of God is eternal life in Christ Jesus our Lord."

Romans 6:23 ESV

I have a package for you! But first let me tell you a story. I was concerned about a package that I was supposed to get, and it was so critical going into the Christmas week. My friend made a promise that the package would be sent overnight, and I had to be there the next afternoon to receive it. I waited for confirmation, and the message was the package is sent and there was a tracking number! The tracking number is critical because if you log in to the deliverers website and enter the number you can see the progress of your package. So, I did that and saw the movement of the package from state to state, then city to city. I waited with anticipation for the package to arrive, however, I could not wait around and do nothing, so I had to occupy my time until the package came. I cleaned my house and I got some work done for myself. I was very productive, and I felt very accomplished, and then it happened, the knock at the door. The package came, and I was excited. However, to receive the package I had to sign for it because it could not be left at my door for me to pick up later. I'm so glad I waited for it.

I said before, I have a package for you! And this package has a tracking number. If you fancy to know the status of this package you just use the tracking number and you will be encouraged to see that it is going from state to state, city to city, country to country. Are you ready for it? The tracking number is Romans

6:23. This gift is called everlasting life, and it has a lifetime warranty. It is coming soon you can count on it. Yet, stay productive until it comes and get your house in order. You will soon hear the knock at the door. Now this gift of everlasting life is something that you are required to sign for. The package cannot be left at the door for you to come back and get it later. If you don't sign for it the deliverer will take it back to its origination. I have a package for you! Will you accept?

CALL FAILURE DEVOTION

However, the hair of his head began to grow again after it had been shaven.

Judges 16:22 NKJV

I just bought the iPhone X. It is definitely an upgrade to my iPhone 6. It's fast, takes better pics and holds more data. These pics are phenomenal, no matter where I am, it makes me look like I took a professional pic. Even my streaming is clearer. I am truly appreciating my iPhone upgrade. However, no matter how advanced the technology is, the moment I go through a territory with no reception, my calls drop the same! The finer technical phone still tells me that I've had a call failure. I've come to realize, it is not the phone, it is the service. If I go through an area where there is no service provider, then I can't do much with the new improved phone! The phone is depending on the outside source to bring its connection.

Samson was a human upgrade! The Bible doesn't really describe him as "Muscle Man" with a 6 pack and large forearms. For all we know, he could've been an average size man, however, what we do know, he had supernatural powers as long as he was connected to the Holy Spirit. He turned into Hulk with the Spirit as his power source. He was called by God to be a superhero for Israel, defeating large armies and representing the kingdom of God. He was stronger than any man until he met Delilah, she was the area where Samson lost his signal. He revealed to her his secret passcode and she destroyed his braided power cord. One day, he requested God-care, and his hair started to grow back.

He reconnected to his power source (God) and his call was restored. I thank God that all dropped calls can be restored even if we need to turn off our device and restart. God has created restoring power in our device. For it is not the device, it is what the device is connected to. Connect with God today and your signal will remain strong!

BEATS, RHYMES, & PHIFE

"A friend is always loyal, and a brother is born to help in time of need."

To the world he was known as Phife Dawg, to those of us who knew him, he was Malik aka "Malik Ski" or "Magic Man". He was a member of the group "A Tribe Called Quest" along with Q-Tip, Ali Shaheed Muhammad and Jarobi. His contributions to the world of Hip Hop are immeasurable. On March 23, 2016 he lost his fight with diabetes.

Between 3am and 4am my sister Sheryl called me with the news of his death! Needless to say, I couldn't sleep. All of the memories I had of Phife go back to Queens, New York, more specifically the Linden SDA School where my sister and many of our friends attended.

Malik met up with a friend formerly known as John Davis, now Q-Tip. They became brothers and their relationship would provide the world with a new flavor in hip-hop music. In 1989, they were given an opportunity from Kool DJ Red Alert, A Tribe Called Quest would take their first musical journey with their first album, The People's Instinctive Travels and the Paths of Rhythm. The first single they released was *Description of a Fool*, although the first video was *I Left My Wallet in El Segundo*. They also formed **Native Tongue** a collaboration of De La Soul, Jungle Brothers, Leaders of the New School, Queen Latifah, Monie Love, Brand Nubian, Black Sheep, Mos Def and more. Since then, they have blazed the trails in the style of music infusing jazz and smooth melodies with occasional hard boom rap beats.

Malik was generous and kind. He always had a great outlook on life. Warren Thomas a vocalist from recording group Naturally 7 recalls, "About 12 years ago Malik and I were sitting in his home talking about some of the issues that caused a lot of problems in his group, one main issue was that he didn't convert to Islam. Many in his group and the Hip-Hop community saying "How can I deny Christ? That goes against everything I grew up believing and still believe", and it made him the odd man out, but he stuck to that." Malik was not shy about his conviction. Listening to his interviews over the years he was always committed to being real with himself.

I was an aspiring rap artist as a teen and would visit Malik's grandmother's house. He was with Q-tip searching for the next Tribe song through a crate of records. For some reason vinyl records always fit perfectly in a milk crate from the grocery store. Malik pulled me aside and gave me some advice about the record industry. He told me it was fun being in the studio and performing on stage, however there were more headaches to follow with shady managers, record executives and more. He didn't discourage me, yet he gave me enough to think about before I went any further with my ambition to become a rap artist!

Today I still hold the mic, just as a preacher, people still hold their hands in the air too. I guess God has a funny way of speaking to us all. I appreciate how Q-Tip, Phife and Jarobi still found a way to show their people love and concern. Karen Pilgrim, who along with her brother Curtis Pilgrim were great friends of Malik reminiscence, "My greatest Memory of Malik was in 1987, I suggested with some other friends and fans that Malik and Brian Johnson perform for Queens Youth Federation Day as Christian Rappers. Aunt Denise

Dolland was known for being a fun loving, hip, support to young people's talents. So, the day of the event came, my aunt introduced them; then THE BEAT BOX BEGAN.

Malik said, "Throw your hands in the air, and wave them like you just don't care and if you love Jesus say oh yea, oh yea!"

They had everybody on their feet and Malik killed his rhyme, Brian killed his rhyme and Aunt Denise couldn't get the mic from them. They had youth federation pumping. That was a historical memory when Malik and Brian brought rap to the church.

Looking back, I am more sensitive to youth today and how they express themselves. Brian Johnson says, "He was the first person I knew that would use the Gospel in his rhymes and made it sound good."

The life of Phife reveals to us the joy and pain of purpose. He fought through diabetes, he fought through a career shift, and nothing sustained him more than his fight and will to live. His wife Deisha Taylor was a major part to sustaining his life when she gifted him with her kidney. A moment we witnessed from Michael Rappaport's documentary about A Tribe Called Quest, Beats, Rhymes, and Life. Since 1990, Malik had been dealing with diabetes. In the 90's there weren't many healthy options. As I contemplated his death, I thought about my battle with diabetes and those around me who have died way too early because of health issues. Therefore I am constantly working on changes in how I eat.

This was his life. The good, bad, and all with purpose. He impacted the hip-hop world so much that they did Phife Medley's on the radio, The New York Jets have his team jersey on display and the Apollo theatre memorialized his legacy. There are many more like Malik, in and out of the church. They have a voice, and some use it and some abuse it. I believe it is our duty as a church to pray for people even if we don't agree with their life choices. We can still pray for individuals and see how God continues to work in their lives.

Thanks to Jason Kibble, who inspired me to write this thought. Shout outs to Pastors Paul and Patrick Graham, Quest Green, DJs who did the Phife Medley on all radio stations and many more!

Now our friend is laid to rest but his memory lives on. Is there a friend that you need to pray for? Pray with? Make that move now! I am praying for you on stage and off the stage! The greatest contract we will ever sign is one with God. Pursue a life with Him and heaven will be your Award Tour!

SAY WHAT YOU MEAN

"But what do you think? A man had two sons, and he came to the first and said, 'Son, go, work today in my vineyard.' He answered and said, 'I will not,' but afterward he regretted it and went. Then he came to the second and said likewise. And he answered and said, 'I go, sir,' but he did not go. Which of the two did the will of his father?"

Matthew 21:28-31 NKJV

If people would say what they mean and mean what they say, there would be a lot less confusion in the world. We exist in a society where it's easily said, but not always easily done. Many of us like to impress others with our words; however, we often create personas that we can't live up to when it's time to produce. As a teenager, I wanted to be a rap artist so I learned a lot about words. Often, the lyrics in rap songs and even the rappers' names build them up to be larger than they really are. With their lyrics, rappers have abilities and powers that very few of us enjoy. Why? In the Garden of Eden, words impressed Eve enough to give up living forever in exchange for knowledge of good and evil. You see, she understood evil because of her experiences. A mere ninety-five lines of words written on the door of the German Catholic Church by Martin Luther in 1517 started a major protest. In addition, powerful words by the late Reverend Dr. Martin Luther King Jr., spoken before about 250,000 people and televised nationally on Aug. 28, 1963, expressed a dream for freedom from racism and equality for all. Books are written, songs are sung and the wonderful words of life are ingrained into the mind of listeners. Yet, do all the words that are written or sung truly mean what they say?

I've met tons of politicians who come to small towns and big cities and excite people by their words, only to find that months later their actions don't line up with what they said they were going to do for those from whom they sought votes. There are some politicians, and people in general, who know what they can provide and stick to that course of action. Trust me when I tell you that it's very important to do what you say you're going to do, to be a person of integrity, because people will be far more impressed by your deliverance on promises than the big words you spew when you talk, or "boast" about what you're going to do. None of us, no matter who we are, can do much with empty promises. When you say what you mean, people know exactly what to expect from you. When your actions reflect your words, people have an easier time making decisions. If you confuse people with a bunch of words, in other words, if you're all talk and no action, people will have a hard time reading you. Try to live your life in such a way that your words are expressed with clarity and your actions match your words.

After years of talking and listening, I've started taking actions over talk. The reality is I can't control what you say to me, but I can control how long I put up with your hot air!

THE MINISTRY OF PRESENCE

And I was with you in weakness, and in fear, and in much trembling.

1 Corinthians 2:3 NKJV

When something tragic happens to a family member or friend, we suddenly become like deer in the proverbial headlights in terms of what to do next. We aren't sure what to say during sad moments in our friends' lives. Oftentimes, because we don't want to say something stupid or awkward, we're left speechless. Then, before we know it, we blurt out, "I'm sorry." When we're really feeling hopeless, we usually also say, "I understand what you're going through," when, in reality, we don't know what that person is going through. Even if your friend has just lost his or her mother and your mother already passed away, you still don't know what your friend is going through. Each of us grieves in our own way. Likewise, you might have been very close to your mother and had a loving relationship with her; meanwhile your friend might be trying to remember the last time he or she bothered to pick up the phone to call his or her mother. If that's the case, your friend is probably experiencing guilt on top of sadness. That said, I'd like to encourage you to encourage others with your presence.

You may be wondering what I mean. It's simple. The ministry of presence is just that – presence. Sometimes a friend doesn't need advice from you, or your take on the best solution to his or her problem. Sometimes, in the moment, all your friend needs is for you to be there, providing a shoulder to cry on, or a listening ear. Your friend may simply need someone to walk with him or her through the journey. The ministry of presence is so powerful, and it's far better than all the advice that we can give. Just being there, being present and showing up when needed is a very powerful ministry indeed!

You can say what you want about Job's friends, but they showed up when he really needed them. The attack Job was experiencing was rare, and the truth is, his friends didn't know how to cope with it. Even Job's wife didn't know what to say. Yet we know they stuck with him until the very end. We can learn a lot from Job's friends regarding what to say and what not to say. They had a powerful ministry of presence that rendered them equipped for the job when they really didn't know what to do or what to say.

Have you struggled with what to say to a friend who's going through? Well, here's the good news: You may not need to say anything at all. Sometimes, just being present is enough. Sometimes, just showing up is enough. Sometimes, you can say a whole lot by saying nothing at all!

#AUTHORS

Paula Blackwell

Paula is native of Birmingham, Alabama. She and her husband Redell live in Houston, Texas. Paula is the daughter of a Minister and Nurse Practitioner. Paula graduated from Bass Memorial Academy and later attended Oakwood College (now Oakwood University). In 1989, tragically, her parents were in a near fatal car accident and she came home from college to care for them. As Paula was caring for her parents, her mother encouraged her to return to a local college to finish her degree. In 1991, she enrolled in Stillman College as a junior. Paula decided that she only wanted to go to Stillman if they would give her permission to take all of her classes in one year. The administration at Stillman College agreed. Paula finished 2 years of college in one year. She was determined to finish all of her classes in one year. She graduated with honors from Stillman in 1992. Paula also holds a Master's degree in Education from Walden University.

Today, she is a writer, educator, and entrepreneur. Paula is a self-proclaimed serial entrepreneur. In her short lifetime, she has owned a children's bookstore, and helped launch several non-profit organizations. She considers herself a life strategist; she helps women recraft their lives. Paula is a woman passionate about faith and prayer. Paula is the eldest daughter of Arthur and Carrie Sanders. She has one Sister Pamela Sanders. She is the mother to twin daughters Mauriah Danielle Morris and Maiah Denene Morris. She is the happy stepmother to Traci and DeSean Blackwell and is the Grandmother "Mimi" to three beautiful kids KaMel Blackwell, Alana Williams, and Maurice Yancy.

Kymone Hinds

Kymone Hinds is an international speaker, author, life coach and minister who knows what it takes to help leaders bring Ideas to Life. Kymone pastored for over 15 years and had a special gift for reaching youth and young adults. His passion is helping younger generations to live out their full potential as followers of Christ. His first book was titled "This is Church...Where you fit in." Kymone now resides in Florida with his family. He is living out the call of God to minister to others as an entrepreneur.

You can connect with Kymone via his website: w w w . K y m o n e H i n d s . c o m .

Philip M. Wesley, II

Philip M. Wesley, II is a native of Long Island, New York. He is a father of two, Shaniya Josephine and Leah Gabriele. After attending a year at Oakwood University (formerly Oakwood College), Pastor Wesley graduated from Atlantic Union College with degrees in Communication and Religion. He then continued his education at the Theological Seminary at Andrews University where he obtained his Master of Divinity Degree. Currently he is a Phd Student studying Business Administration at the University of Montemorelos.

He is the CEO/President of McGuire Entertainment Group, a marketing group for Christian Artists and Atlantic Union College Alumni President. He also is a writer for Message Magazine with his column, Elevation: Media That Takes You Higher.

Pastor Wesley has held a number of leadership roles in the ministry. Among them, he served as the Youth/Associate Pastor at the Ephesus SDA Church in Harlem, NY, Pastor of the Friendship SDA Church in Elmira, NY, and the Associate Youth Director for the Northeastern Conference.

Pastor Wesley has served as the Pastor of the New Dimension and Triumphant Tabernacle Seventh-day Adventist Church in Brooklyn, NY. While serving in Brooklyn, he was a sector leader with the 67th Precinct Clergy Council, helping to address gun violence in the community. Currently he is the Pastor of the Mt. Olive SDA Church in New London, CT and Emmanuel SDA Church in Providence, Rhode Island where he is an advocate with the Community Chaplain's Corp.

CPSIA information can be obtained
at www.ICGtesting.com
Printed in the USA
BVHW040821090420
577268BV00008B/207

9 781948 877169